Ohio Statehouse

A Building for the Ages

Chris Kasson, Ohio Department of Development

Nov. 15th 2011

Ohio Statehouse
A Building for the Ages

To Robin and Richard,
I hope you enjoy
our book!

Cheryl J. Straker

Cheryl J. Straker and Chris Matheney

Chris Matheney

CAPITOL SQUARE
REVIEW AND
ADVISORY BOARD

The
OHIO STATEHOUSE
MUSEUM
EDUCATION CENTER

THE
DONNING COMPANY
PUBLISHERS

The Donning Company Publishers
184 Business Park Drive, Suite 206
Virginia Beach, VA 23462

Steve Mull, General Manager
Barbara Buchanan, Office Manager
Pamela Koch, Senior Editor
Lori Wiley, Graphic Designer
Priscilla Odango, Imaging Artist
Susan Adams, Project Research Coordinator
Tonya Washam, Marketing Specialist
Pamela Engelhard, Marketing Advisor

Ed Williams, Project Director

Library of Congress Cataloging-in-Publication Data

Straker, Cheryl J., 1960–
  Ohio Statehouse : a building for the ages / Cheryl J. Straker and Chris Matheney.
      p. cm.
  ISBN 978-1-57864-682-1 (soft cover : alk. paper)
 1. Ohio Statehouse (Columbus, Ohio) 2. Ohio Statehouse (Columbus, Ohio)—Pictorial works. 3. Capitol Square District (Columbus, Ohio) 4. Capitol Square District (Columbus, Ohio)—Pictorial works. 5. Columbus (Ohio)—Buildings, structures, etc. 6. Columbus (Ohio)—Buildings, structures, etc.—Pictorial works. I. Matheney, Chris, 1965- II. Title.
  F499.C780467 2011
  977.1'57—dc22
                          2011009787

Printed in the United States of America at
Walsworth Publishing Company

Table of Contents

Foreword

Over the years, people have consistently asked whether we had a book about the Ohio Statehouse. They wanted something to take home with them to remember this temple to Ohio democracy. Now it is here.

The writing and photos assembled here give one a graphic picture of the Capitol Square complex and grounds. It puts on paper what the tour guides and others show you in person. It is truly a story of this wonderful building that has been restored to its original grandeur and is the envy of our sister states. Ohioans can be very proud of their capitol building that has been serving as the heart of Ohio democracy for more than 150 years.

I wish to commend authors Cheryl Straker and Chris Matheney for their willingness and commitment to see this project to completion. I think you will find it rewarding.

Senator Richard H. Finan
Chairman
Capitol Square Review and Advisory Board

Preface

When the Ohio Statehouse was completed in 1861, Ohioans joined together to contemplate the wonder of the monumental achievement that resulted in this centerpiece of Ohio democracy. The Ohio Statehouse stands at the center of Capitol Square and at the center of public life for Ohioans. With its Greek revival architecture, it is one of the most historically and symbolically significant buildings in our nation. Ohio's Capitol is both the seat of state government and a political symbol of our democratic heritage, spirit, and accomplishments as a self-governing people.

The identity of a people is shaped by their history, their symbols, and their shared experiences. Ohio's Capitol is a fundamentally important part of that shared identity and heritage. This complex provides a sense of identity and continuity among past, present, and future generations of Ohioans.

This book provides the opportunity to reflect on the building's history and the great men and women who have come to serve the people. As you peruse these pages, you will discover the beauty of the building and the symbolism that has inspired Ohioans.

William E. Carleton
Executive Director
Capitol Square Review and Advisory Board

Acknowledgments

Capitol Square Review and Advisory Board (CSRAB)
Senator Richard Finan, Board Chairman
William E. Carleton, Executive Director
Barry Hayden, Educational Services Manager
Gregg Dodd, Deputy Director Communications, Marketing, and Events
Mike Rupert, Communications Specialist
Luke Stedke, Volunteer Coordinator

Columbus Landmarks Foundation
Kathy Mast Kane, Executive Director
Doreen Uhas Sauer, President

Columbus Metropolitan Library
Andrew Miller, Local History Librarian
Nick Taggart, Library Assistant

Ohio Legislative Service Commission Library
Debbie Tavenner, Library Administrator

Paul V. Galvin Library Illinois Institute of Technology
Paul Go, Systems Librarian/Library Technology Manager

Ohio Government Telecommunications (OGT)
Dan Shellenbarger, Executive Director

Ohio Historical Society (OHS)
Aaron O'Donovan, Curator of Digital Collections
Elizabeth Nelson, Head, Special Projects Department

Schooley Caldwell Associates (SCA)—*Architect of the Capitol*
Robert D. Loversidge, Jr., FAIA, President/CEO
Jayne Vandenburgh, Vice President/COO

State Library of Ohio
Cheryl Lubow
Audrey Hall

Toledo Museum of Art
Timothy Motz

John and Janet Waldsmith

Welcome

Standing in stark contrast to Columbus' modern urban skyline, the Ohio Statehouse gleams like an ancient Classical-age temple. Constructed of local Ohio limestone, the historic Ohio Statehouse, Senate Building, and modern Atrium rest in simple, monochromatic grandeur on a beautifully landscaped ten-acre plot collectively known as Capitol Square.

The Statehouse is listed on the National Register of Historic Places and is a designated National Historic Landmark.

A major renovation of Capitol Square took place from 1990 to 1996 to return the Ohio Statehouse and Senate Building to their original stateliness. The Statehouse as originally constructed contained 53 rooms; by 1986 that number had grown to 317. The resulting maze of overcrowded offices, cramped hallways, and blocked exits created the epitome of safety hazards. The Senate Building's grand marble staircase and captivating murals were soiled with smoke and dirt. Over the decades, each new generation carried out a haphazard series of renovations that ultimately marred the buildings' tasteful elegance and left behind an incoherent jumble of differing styles.

State Senator Richard H. Finan recognized the need for improvement. He consulted with interested colleagues and outside organizations, garnering the necessary support to move forward with a complete renovation. The Capitol Square Renovation Foundation formed to solicit private funds, eventually raising more than $10 million to aid the restoration efforts. The state commissioned Columbus' Schooley Caldwell Associates to create a renovation master plan, which they completed in 1989. The master plan called for work to begin on the

The Statehouse Rotunda and Atrium are popular venues for weddings, receptions, and other special events.

Ellen Dallager Photography

10

Senate Building. While this work was being done, a connector or "stone screen" was added, linking the Annex to the Statehouse. The Atrium, as it is now called, uses architectural elements of both buildings and provides a spacious, elegant location for public events. Once the Senate Building and Atrium were completed, the renovation project moved into its final phase, and work commenced on the Ohio Statehouse. Built in an era in which a genuine American-style architecture first came to light, Ohio's Greek revival Statehouse was fully restored to its original grandeur in 1996.

Housed within the Statehouse's massive walls are the House and Senate Chambers of the Ohio General Assembly, the office of the governor, the ceremonial offices of the state treasurer and auditor, and public hearing rooms. Party caucuses and legislative leadership offices are housed on the upper floors. Legislators and members of the public can pick up information on current bills at the Legislative Service Commission's Bill Room on the ground floor. Amenities are found in the Statehouse Museum Shop, the Capitol Cafe, and the Ohio Travel and Tourism office. Capitol Square Review and Advisory Board, the state agency responsible for maintaining Capitol Square's historic character, oversees the day-to-day operations. The Senate Building houses the state senators' offices and public hearing rooms. The offices for members of the Ohio House of Representatives are located in the Vern Riffe State Office Tower across High Street from the Statehouse.

More than 500,000 people come to Ohio's Capitol Square annually to participate in state government, attend a special event, or view a press conference. The Statehouse Rotunda and Atrium are popular venues for weddings and receptions. Tourists from around the world come to enjoy the Capitol's architectural splendor, take a guided tour, and visit the Ohio Statehouse Museum Education Center.

Visitors from around the world admire the architecture of the Statehouse and enjoy public events.

Top: Capitol Square Review and Advisory Board is the state agency responsible for maintaining the historic character of the Ohio Statehouse.

Ohio Statehouse

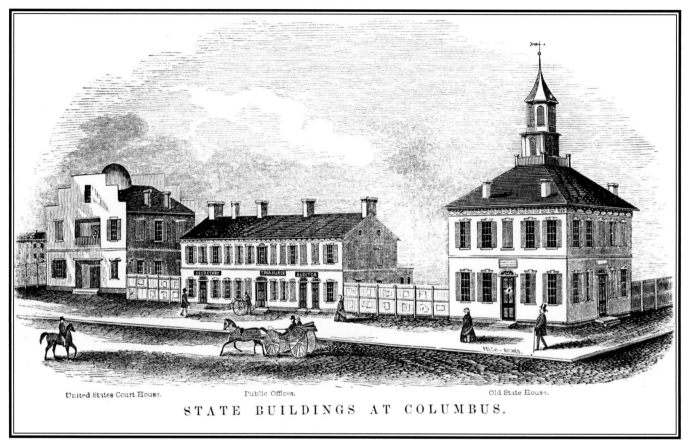

United States Court House.   Public Offices.   Old State House.

STATE BUILDINGS AT COLUMBUS.

The first buildings on Capitol Square: the U.S. Court House, Public Offices, and first Columbus State House (spelled then as two words).

Ohio Historical Society

Bold, noble, and stately, the Ohio Statehouse inspires pride in the state's citizens and elicits praise from national and international visitors. Built in an age when Americans believed that public architecture could shape beliefs, refine discourse, and instill patriotism, the Statehouse symbolizes the solidity and permanence of Ohio's government.

In the early 1800s, four prominent landholders from the nascent town of Franklinton donated a ten-acre square plot of land on the west bank of the Scioto River to the State of Ohio for a new capital. The public square was the site of Columbus' first Capitol building, but not the first state capital. That honor went to Chillicothe, which served as the territorial capital of the eastern portion of the Northwest Territory and as the first state capital when Ohio achieved statehood in 1803. The seat of government moved to Zanesville in 1808, back to Chillicothe in 1810, and finally to Columbus in 1812. Unlike most states that placed their capitals in already established towns, Ohio located its capital in a forested wilderness. Slowly, a town emerged, and the first Columbus Statehouse was completed in 1816. Thomas Worthington, known as the "Father of Statehood" for his determined fight for Ohio to become the nation's seventeenth state, was the first governor to occupy the new "State House" (it was then two words).

As the town and the state slowly matured in the first quarter of the nineteenth century, government functions expanded, increasing the number of state offices. Addressing the Ohio General Assembly in 1837, Governor Jeremiah Morrow remarked, "Our present State Office buildings are not only

Ohio Governor Jeremiah Morrow

Ohio Historical Society

inconvenient, but much exposed, and liable to destruction by fire." The legislature took notice and passed a joint resolution on January 26, 1838, authorizing the construction of a new Statehouse on the public square in Columbus.

A three-man Board of Commissioners immediately contracted with a local quarry owner to procure the necessary limestone for the contemplated Statehouse and circulated a call for designs in Ohio, New York City, Philadelphia, and Washington, D.C. Receiving fifty to sixty designs by the October deadline, the commissioners awarded the top three prizes: the first-place design by Henry Walter of Cincinnati received $500;

> **There has been no sum fixed for the cost of the State House; but we believe that in the general style, convenience, and durability of her Capitol, Ohio does not wish to be second to any State in the Union.**
>
> **The Grecian Doric Order is suggested, but not with a view of governing exclusively in the choice.**
>
> *Excerpt from the Statehouse Commissioners' 1838 circular setting forth design requirements for the new Ohio Statehouse*

followed by Martin E. Thomas of New York City, $300; and Thomas Cole of Catskill, New York, $200.

The three chosen designs all employed the Greek revival style, but with significant variations. Unable to agree on a final plan, the commissioners sought the aid of New York architect Alexander Jackson Davis. Davis made finished drawings of each of the three award-winning plans. The final plan was a composite modification of the top three designs showing elements of Cole's entry.

The commissioners prepared cost estimates and recommended employing experienced stone-cutting convicts from the nearby Ohio Penitentiary to save on labor wages. In the spring of 1839, workers erected an office, a storeroom, and a high fence around a portion of the square to

Thomas Cole, best known as a landscape painter, sketched his plan for the Ohio Statehouse on the envelope in which he received the circular calling for the submission of plans.

New York State Library

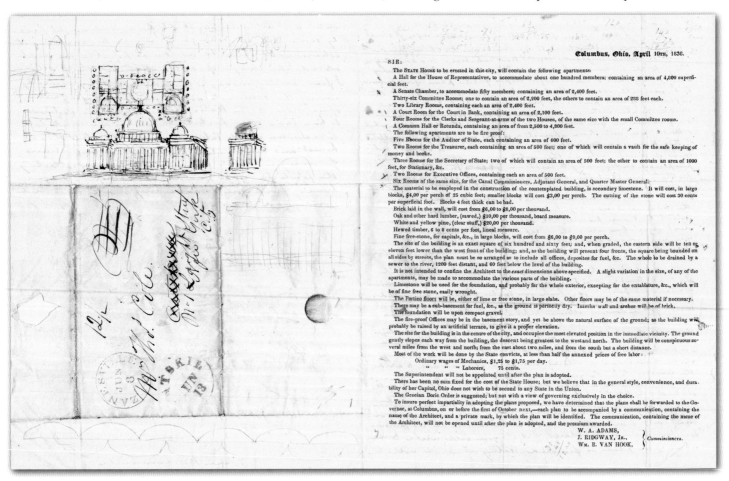

14

The Architect's Dream

Thomas Cole's painting illustrates his serious interest in architecture and vividly captures the romantic mood that influenced American art and architecture in the mid-1800s. What has been called the "cult of the classical" was part of the romantic tradition, and it is clearly evident in the many forms of classical architecture present in Cole's composition.

Thomas Cole (American, born England, 1801–1848), The Architect's Dream, 1840, oil on canvas, 53 x 84 1/16 in., Toledo Museum of Art (Toledo, Ohio), Purchased with funds from the Florence Scott Libbey Bequest in Memory of her Father, Maurice A. Scott, 1949.162.

Photo Credit: Image Source, Toledo Museum of Art.

FELLOW CITIZENS—On this day, the anniversary of American Independence, the foundation of a great edifice is to be laid; you are assembled to witness and assist in the interesting ceremonies; an edifice that will be dedicated as a Temple of Law—the Capitol of the State. . . .

Let the foundations be deep and strong; let the materials be of nature's most lasting gifts—durable—imperishable; let the edifice rise in solemn, simple grandeur, a monument of chaste and classic beauty. . . . And May the councils of truth and justice and public virtue preside in its halls; may discord and faction be put far from them; and may a free and united people, who reared it, and whose temple it is, watch over and cherish within its wall the form and spirit of their republican institutions. And

I now lay the cornerstone of the Capitol of Ohio!

Former Ohio governor Jeremiah Morrow's closing remarks at the laying of the new Statehouse cornerstone, July 4, 1839

prevent prisoners from escaping. The hard work of excavating and laying the foundation began under the eye of architect Henry Walter, and by early summer, all was ready for laying the Statehouse cornerstone.

With much fanfare and ceremony, city and state officials, veterans, militia groups, and more than five thousand citizens witnessed the cornerstone laid into place. Neither the dignitaries nor the public could have known that another twenty-two years would pass before the Statehouse was declared finished. A prolonged

Tightly shackled convicts are seen on the grounds of the Ohio Penitentiary circa 1858. Inmates from "the Pen" performed much of the hard labor on the construction of the Ohio Statehouse.

Ohio Historical Society F. & R. Lazarus Collection

and aggressive campaign over moving the capital to another location, a deadly cholera outbreak, and the legislature's refusal to appropriate necessary funding halted or delayed work from 1840 to 1848. The half-finished foundation was covered over and became a grassy pasture.

When construction finally resumed in 1848, the commissioners, superintendents, architects, and legislators squabbled over design and construction details. Spanning nearly a decade, arguments ensued over whether prison laborers should be employed; whether the interior finishes were too elaborate; whether the staircases were structurally sound; whether costs exceeded estimates; whether contractors were corrupt—the list of complaints seemed to never end. A suspicious fire destroyed the first Columbus Statehouse in the winter of 1852, providing the impetus and motivation to complete construction on the new Capitol.

Inmate Ephraim Badger, incarcerated for burglary at the "State Pen" from 1846 to 1849, left his mark on the stone foundation with a self-portrait.

These are two of most whimsical pieces of graffiti left behind by the prisoners who constructed the Statehouse. One is signed "Badger"; the other is unsigned or is now illegible, but they are believed to have been done by the same hand.

Ohio Government
Telecommunications

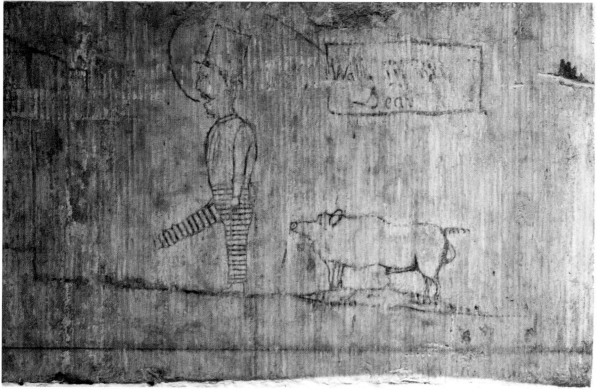

Governor's office

By 1857 the governor's office and legislative chambers were ready for occupancy. Addressing the Fifty-Second Ohio General Assembly, Governor Salmon P. Chase welcomed House and Senate members with "great pleasure, to the first session of the General Assembly in the New State House. In simplicity of Design, in harmony of Proportions, and in massive solidity of Structure, it stands, and may it long stand, a monument and a symbol of the clear Faith, the well ordered Institutions, and the enduring Greatness of the People whose House it is." A grand celebration accompanied the opening of the new Capitol, complete with a public banquet in the Rotunda and dancing in the House and Senate Chambers.

Renovated and refurnished in the 1990s, the governor's office today appears almost exactly as it did in 1857. The office qualifies as a Zone 1 restoration with light switches, telephones, and computers concealed within the furniture. The desk and bookcase are the original pieces custom designed for the Ohio Statehouse and used by Salmon P. Chase in 1857.

This extremely rare stereograph by J.Q.A. Tresize of Zanesville, Ohio, is the earliest known image of the Statehouse interior. Salmon P. Chase sits at his desk in the governor's office circa 1857.

John and Janet Waldsmith

The governor's office today exhibits the highest level of preservation standards and appears virtually the same as it did when the Statehouse opened in 1857.

This rare stereograph shows Governor Charles Foster's office draped in black crepe to mourn the death of President James A. Garfield in 1881.

John and Janet Waldsmith

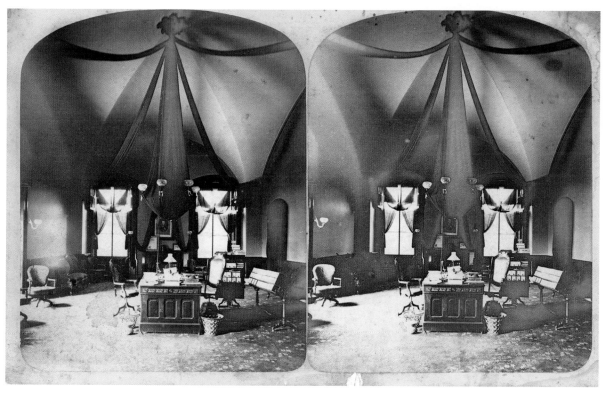

Style and architects

The Statehouse from the corner of Broad and High Streets, circa 1870

Ohio Historical Society F. & R. Lazarus Collection

An example of architect Nathan Kelley's "florid" ornamentation on a column in the House of Representatives

When completed in 1861, the Ohio Statehouse was the second largest building in the nation (the U.S. Capitol being the largest). Built in the understated and uncomplicated Greek revival style popular in America at the time, the Statehouse expressed the much-admired qualities of simplicity and rationality. The style harkened back to Ancient Greece—the first democracy in the Western world—and reflected the principles of liberty, freedom, and equality. Then and now, it is considered one of the finest Greek revival–style buildings in the country. Architect Frank Lloyd Wright pronounced it "the most honest of all American Statehouses."

The design of the Ohio Statehouse cannot be attributed to any one individual; five principal architects contributed ideas and improvements throughout the years. Nathan B. Kelley (third architect 1854–1858) was responsible for many of the interior details enjoyed by visitors today. Kelley favored "florid" ornamentation, deemed excessive, inappropriate, and incompatible in his time with the Greek revival style, causing him to be fired from the project.

The Ohio General Assembly

Thirty-three state senators and ninety-nine state representatives comprise the bicameral Ohio General Assembly. The legislators meet separately in their respective chambers to debate and ultimately to vote on legislation. Legislators' desks in the House and Senate are reproductions of the originals and have been modified with microphones, telephones, and computers. Most of the woodwork in both chambers is original; the paint colors are reproductions of the originals. The marble daises used by the Speaker of the House and the Senate President are also original.

Legislators in the Ohio House vote electronically with the results tallied on two screens on each side of the chamber. Senators approve or reject legislation verbally in an alphabetic roll call vote.

Above: This view of the House Chamber was taken from the balcony, which provides public seating for visitors.

Only members of the House of Representatives and their senior staff are permitted on the House Chamber floor.

Schooley Caldwell Associates

The Speaker of the House is the highest-ranking legislator in the Ohio House of
Representatives; the Speaker's office is located on the second floor of the Ohio Statehouse.

Ohio Government Telecommunications

The Ohio House Members' Lounge is located in one of the former Statehouse light courts.

Ohio Government Telecommunications

A view of the Senate Chamber shows the desks of Ohio's thirty-three state senators; the blue sofas lining the inside perimeter are used by Senate aides. The seating visible on the left is for public visitors.

The Senate president is the highest-ranking legislator in the Ohio Senate. The Senate president's office is located on the second floor of the Ohio Statehouse.

Ohio Government Telecommunications

The Ohio Senate Members' Lounge is located in one of the former Statehouse light courts.

Light Courts

Sunlight streaming through the top of light courts provided natural light to the interior rooms of the Statehouse. Glass ceilings now top the courts, which were originally uncovered and open to the weather.

Ohio Government Telecommunications

The Statehouse was designed before the use of indoor gas lighting (although when completed twenty-two years later it was fairly common). Rooms located along the building's exterior walls had tall windows to let in sunlight. Four open courtyards—or light courts—created false exteriors that allowed sunlight to enter through the top of the building down to the inner rooms. When electric lighting was added to the Statehouse, the need for light courts diminished. As state government grew and office space became precious, the light courts were viewed as prime real estate. One courtyard eventually contained seven floors crammed with hastily constructed offices.

The original Ohio Statehouse boasted indoor plumbing, which was relatively uncommon in 1861. Limestone balconies crossed the light courts, leading from meeting rooms and offices to restrooms, or "water closets." Additional water closets were added near the House Chamber in 1876, when the sewer lines were accidentally connected to the building's ventilation ducts. The air in the Statehouse, especially near the House Chamber, grew particularly nauseating. Newspaper reports from the period refer to the stench and ensuing problems as "Statehouse Malaria." After eight long years, the problem was finally diagnosed, and 150 barrels of filth were removed from the ducts.

Today, two light courts have been fully reopened and contain glass-walled elevators. The remaining light courts contain the Ohio House and Senate Members' lounges.

Presidential Hearing Rooms

The Ulysses S. Grant Presidential Hearing Room honors the eighteenth U.S. president (1869–1877), who was born in Point Pleasant, Ohio. A graduate of West Point, Grant served as General in Chief of the Union Army and forced Confederate General Robert E. Lee's surrender in April 1865 to end the Civil War.

Ohio Government Telecommunications

Beginning in the early 1840s and nearly dominating the latter half of the nineteenth and early twentieth centuries, eight men from Ohio held the nation's highest executive office. To this day, a friendly rivalry exists between Ohio and Virginia, both of which vie for the title "Mother of Presidents." Each state claims eight U.S. presidents as their own, sharing William Henry Harrison, who was born in Virginia but was elected president while living in Ohio.

Used by House or Senate legislative committees to hear public testimony on bills under consideration, eight of the Statehouse hearing rooms are named in honor of Ohio presidents—many of whom served as state legislators or governor. Each room features a portrait of the president and historic artifacts related to their private and professional lives.

The William Howard Taft Presidential Hearing Room honors the nation's twenty-seventh president (1909–1913), a native of Cincinnati. Taft also served as a U.S. Supreme Court Chief Justice and Secretary of War.

Ohio Government Telecommunications

State Room

The State Room provides meeting space and a venue for press conferences and events.

Ohio Government Telecommunications

The State Room contains 1860s period furnishings and serves as a meeting room, a site for press conferences, and a venue for special events. Likenesses of early Ohio governors from the Statehouse Portrait Collection are displayed in nineteenth-century *salon* style along the walls. The genesis of the portrait collection formed during Governor Rutherford B. Hayes' administration in the 1870s. Governors' portraits are located throughout hearing rooms and Statehouse offices.

George Washington Williams Memorial Room

The George Washington Williams Memorial Room honors Ohio's first African American state legislator. Elected to represent the citizens of Hamilton County in 1879, Williams served one term in the Ohio House of Representatives (1880–1881).

In 2001, Columbus artist Ron Anderson created a painting to illustrate Representative Williams addressing the Ohio House of Representatives in 1880. Located in the southwest corner of the first floor of the Statehouse, the period-furnished room features photographs of late-nineteenth-century African-American state legislators and a searchable computer kiosk listing all black legislators who have served in the Ohio General Assembly.

Artist Ed Dwight created a bust of George Washington Williams in 2001.

Ohio Government Telecommunications

Ladies' Gallery

The Ladies' Gallery interprets the history of women's suffrage and honors female legislators. A portrait of Nancy Hollister—former state legislator and the first woman to serve as Ohio's governor—also hangs in the gallery.

Ohio Government Telecommunications

The passage of the Nineteenth Amendment to the U.S. Constitution in 1920 granted American women the right to vote. In 1922, Ohioans elected six women to the state legislature. The Statehouse Ladies' Gallery is dedicated to those six groundbreaking female legislators and honors all women who have served in the Ohio General Assembly.

Located in the southeast corner of the first floor of the Statehouse, the Ladies' Gallery is used for press conferences, meetings, and visitor education. A panel exhibit chronicles the history of Ohio women's fight for equal rights and women's suffrage. A changing exhibit of historic artifacts showcases accomplishments and the everyday lives of female state legislators.

The State Library Room was demolished when it moved from the Statehouse in the 1930s. The State Library is presently located on First Avenue in Columbus.

Ohio Historical Society

Relic Room

Shortly after the end of the Civil War, Governor Jacob D. Cox designated a third-floor room in the Statehouse as a repository for Ohio regimental and other military flags. Veteran George Slack of the Twenty-Sixth Regiment Ohio Volunteer Infantry—referred to as the "one-armed soldier," having lost his right arm at the Battle of Chickamauga—served as the Flag Room's first caretaker. Considered a "must-see" destination when visiting the Statehouse, the Flag Room inspired awe and reverence in those too well acquainted with the ravages of the war. A report of the Statehouse superintendent captured the feeling:

> *The visitors include every age, every race, and every calling. The lisping four-year-old who comes with dim mysterious feeling to kiss the folds of the flag beneath which his father died, and the gray-haired old man of seventy who spends half the day in climbing the stairway to press to his lips the splintered staff, shattered by the bullet that killed his boy; the mulatto boy who played the cook to some favored officer, and slyly played the hero, too, with rifle matched to his master's sword; the quiet old lady whose black bonnet tells to her acquaintances the story of a son and grandson lost in battle; the young widow who bids her little boy kneel at the foot of the battle flag of the "Old Thirteenth"; the straight up and down old soldier who unconsciously removes his hat and salutes as he catches a glimpse of "our flag"; the color bearer who lost an arm holding "that flag"; the colonel who commanded the day "that staff was shattered"—these and such as these are the visitors to the Flag Room.*

A "Trophy Room" was created in 1868 across the hall from the Flag Room. Veterans and visitors arrived with an odd assortment of military uniforms, weapons, pioneer relics, old money, foreign and ethnological specimens, and curiosities like an old jar of desiccated apples from the late eighteenth century. By the 1880s the name changed to the "Relic Room." Entering visitors signed a guest register, and in 1897 nearly 96,000 people toured the Flag and Relic Rooms, which were also popular with honeymooners.

After years of discussion and planning, the state transferred the accumulated collection of nearly 1,177 relics from the Statehouse to the Ohio Archaeological and History Society (now the Ohio Historical Society) in 1916 where it is now stored.

This is an extremely rare image of the Statehouse Relic Room from the late nineteenth century.

Ohio Historical Society

Rotunda

The central, raised Rotunda is a ceremonial and symbolic space that evokes respect for Ohio history and the accomplishments of its citizens. Over the years, the Rotunda has been the site of celebrations, such as governors' inaugural ceremonies, and mourning, as when President Abraham Lincoln laid in state while thousands passed by in grief.

The focal point of the Rotunda is a magnificent mosaic floor ingeniously laid with hand-cut marble tiles that swirl out from its circular center. A skylight 128 feet above the Rotunda floor features a hand-painted reproduction of the 1847 Great State Seal of Ohio in use when the Statehouse was completed. Limestone and marble staircases on the north and south ends lead up to the House and Senate Chambers.

A view of the Rotunda from the east balcony

An unusual view from above shows the eight niches and intricate marble floor of the Statehouse Rotunda.

Ohio Government Telecommunications

A staff interpreter interacts with students in the Rotunda.

Cupola

Skylight

Ohio Government Telecommunications

In the long span throughout construction and completion, the design of the Statehouse changed many times. A well-known Cincinnati architect, Isaiah Rogers, was hired to supervise the final stages of the Statehouse construction. During his tenure, Rogers oversaw work on the building's interior and coordinated work on the distinctive Rotunda and its enclosing cupola. In opting for a cupola rather than a dome, Rogers reverted to a design scheme proposed by earlier Statehouse architects William Russell West and J. O. Sawyer. Today the cupola is one of the most curious and distinctive features of the Statehouse.

A view of the Statehouse Cupola through a light court (top) and through the trees (above).

The cupola has a circular observation area that surrounds the curving outer wall of the Rotunda (seen at right).

Artwork of the Rotunda

Perry's Victory

The first painting commissioned by the Ohio General Assembly (1857) for the Statehouse commemorates Oliver Hazard Perry's victory against the British on Lake Erie during the War of 1812. The pivotal Lake Erie battle in September 1813 pitted the British lake fleet against the American freshwater fleets. American Commander Perry met the British off the Bass Islands and soundly defeated them; the victory effectively gave control of the lake to the United States. Perry is famous for his written statement, "We have met the enemy and they are ours."

Perry (1785–1819) and his brother, James Alexander Perry, are central in the dinghy. The African American man is Hannibal, Perry's personal servant. More than fifteen percent of Perry's crew was African American. The identities of the other figures are in dispute.

Because of a disagreement over payment with the Ohio legislature, Powell exhibited the painting in other locations before bringing it to Columbus in 1865. Powell later produced a similar painting, *The Battle of Lake Erie*, which hangs in the Senate Wing of the U.S. Capitol building.

Title: Perry's Victory
Artist: William Henry Powell (1823–1879), Ohio
Dates: Commissioned 1857; exhibited 1865
Media: Oil on canvas
Size: 14 feet by 18 feet

Ohio Government Telecommunications

The Signing of the Treaty of Green Ville

The Signing of the Treaty of Green Ville represents a key moment in Ohio statehood. The 1795 treaty between Native Americans and the United States allowed settlers into the territory below the treaty line near Green Ville. After defeat at the Battle of Fallen Timbers a year prior, Little Turtle and other native leaders met "Mad" Anthony Wayne at Fort Greene Ville, now Greenville, Ohio. Little Turtle offers a wampum belt, and The Sun signs the treaty document. Tarhe, The Crane, holds a peace pipe, or calumet.

Howard Chandler Christy grew up in Duncan Falls, Ohio, and became a well-known painter. He moved to New York and became known for his "Christy Girls" (similar to Gibson Girls), the first of which he created in his early twenties for the November 1895 edition of *The Century Magazine.* He is also known for the painting *Scene at the Signing of the Constitution* in Philadelphia. Christy also painted *Dawn of a New Light*, which hangs across from this work in the Statehouse Rotunda.

Title: The Signing of the Treaty of Green Ville
Artist: Howard Chandler Christy (1873–1952), Ohio
Dates: Commissioned January 1945; unveiled August 1945
Media: Oil on canvas attached to board
Size: 22 feet by 17 feet

Ohio Government Telecommunications

Title: Dawn of a New Light

Artist: Howard Chandler Christy (1873–1952), Ohio

Dates: Installed 1950; went to storage 1964;
reinstalled 2001

Media: Oil on canvas

Size: 9 feet by 12 feet

Ohio Government Telecommunications

Dawn of a New Light

Howard Chandler Christy created the painting *Dawn of a New Light* to honor the famous inventor Thomas Edison (1847–1931). A native Ohioan, Edison is shown in three stages of his life: as a home-schooled youth selling newspapers; as a young inventor; and as an adult inventor with more than 1,000 patents.

Inventions such as the phonograph, Ediphone, motion picture, and electric dynamo are represented throughout the painting. The French government presented Edison with a statue, *The Spirit of Life*, which is depicted by the winged figure at the upper left. The statue represented the celebration of Edison's gift to the world—the first practical incandescent electric light bulb. A group of Ohio power companies donated the painting in 1950 to the State of Ohio.

Wilbur and Orville Wright and Their Accomplishments

In 1903, Wilbur and Orville Wright were the first to fly a heavier-than-air, powered airplane. This painting illustrates important places and events in the brothers' lives—their Dayton, Ohio, home and bicycle shop and the site of their historic flight in Kitty Hawk, North Carolina. Their accomplishments include the first airplane flight, and the 909 Signal Corps plane.

Dwight Mutchler, a native Ohioan and art professor at Ohio University, was selected from a group of fifty-two artists to create this painting for the State of Ohio.

Title: Wilbur and Orville Wright and Their Accomplishments
Artist: Dwight Mutchler (1903–1976), Athens, Ohio
Dates: Commissioned 1957; unveiled 1959; put in storage 1964; reinstalled 2004
Media: Oil on canvas
Size: 9 feet by 12 feet

Ohio Government Telecommunications

Lincoln and Soldiers' Monument

Title: Lincoln and Soldiers' Monument

Artist: T. D. Jones (1811–1881), Cincinnati, Ohio

Dates: Commissioned 1865; unveiled 1871

Media: Carrara marble (white) and Quincy granite (black)

Size: 14 feet by 7 feet by 4 feet

Ohio Government Telecommunications

In January 1871, the Ohio General Assembly passed a joint resolution to accept the "Lincoln and Soldiers' Memorial," presented to the state by the Ohio Monument Association. The Association formed immediately after the end of the Civil War and the assassination of President Abraham Lincoln. Executed by Ohio sculptor T. D. Jones, the magnificent marble and granite monument is composed of a bust of Lincoln and a memorial to the Union and Confederate generals present at the Battle of Vicksburg, which took place on July 4, 1863. An elaborately carved central panel shows Confederate officers surrendering under an oak tree to the Union generals (all of whom were from Ohio). Above the base is a quote from Lincoln's second presidential inaugural address, "Care for him who shall have borne the battle and for his widow and his orphans."

Placed in a Rotunda niche, the solemn monument is one of the most popular features of the Statehouse Rotunda. The monument weighs approximately 10,000 pounds.

From left to right:
Confederate officers: Major General John S. Bowen (Commander Bowan's Division), Colonel L. M. Montgomery (Pemberton's aide-de-camp), and Lieutenant General John C. Pemberton (commander Army of Vicksburg)
Union generals: Major General Ulysses S. Grant (commander Army of the Tennessee), Major General James B. McPherson (commander XVII Corps), and Major General William T. Sherman (commander XV Corps)

Museum Gallery

Barrel arches and groin vaults support the weight of the Rotunda floor, located directly above the Museum Gallery.

Ohio Government Telecommunications

Located on the ground floor directly below the Rotunda, the Statehouse Museum Gallery originally housed work areas and large boilers that heated the building. Fear of an explosion caused the boilers to be relocated under the east Statehouse terrace. Today the area is used as a passageway for visitors and legislators entering through the underground parking garage.

The Museum Gallery is also home to the Ohio Statehouse Museum Education Center, which provides an interactive experience to school students and visitors of all ages. The Museum's Introductory Gallery provides an overview to the three branches of Ohio government and highlights the history of Ohio's Constitution. In the Legislative Gallery, visitors learn about the members and leadership of the Ohio General Assembly and can watch oral history interviews by former legislators. The Executive Gallery informs citizens about the budget process, former governors, the governor's cabinet, and annual State of the State addresses. Visitors also learn about how a bill becomes a law and can cast their ballot on contemporary issues facing Ohio.

This stained glass Great Seal of Ohio hung in the Rotunda dome from the 1920s to 1965. In 1989, it was discovered in a Senate Building closet. The seal was restored and placed here in 1996.

The Ohio Statehouse Museum Education Center helps visitors understand Ohio's constitution and the role of state government.

Exhibit Design and Photography by Hilferty & Associates

Abraham Lincoln at the Ohio Statehouse

In 1859, a little-known man from Illinois named Abraham Lincoln addressed a gathering of citizens on the east terrace on the contemporary issues of slavery and Union preservation. A bronze plaque in the Atrium marks the spot where Lincoln spoke.

Governor William Dennison welcomed President-elect Abraham Lincoln in the Statehouse on February 13, 1861. Lincoln stopped in Columbus on his way to the nation's capital. Greeted by a large crowd, Lincoln spoke to a joint session of the Ohio legislature in the House Chamber.

After his death by assassination in 1865, President Lincoln lay in state in the Rotunda where thousands of mourners passed by his casket to pay their respects.

A plaque in the Atrium marks the spot where Lincoln spoke in 1859.

Ohio Government Telecommunications

The Presidential Journey—Reception of the President In The Hall of the Legislature of Columbus, Ohio—The Senate and Legislature In Joint Session.—From a sketch by our Special Artist travelling in the Presidential Train.

Frank Leslie's Illustrated Newspaper, March 2, 1861

Thousands of mourners waited in line to pass by President Lincoln as he lay in state in the Statehouse Rotunda. Notice the columns and windows draped in black crepe, the American flags flying at half staff, and the sign quoting a line from his second inaugural address: With malice to no one [sic], with charity for all.

John and Janet Waldsmith

Mourners of Abraham Lincoln lined the streets of Capitol Square in April 1865. This image shows the funeral procession that accompanied the slain president's body from Union Station to the Statehouse.

Ohio Historical Society

After his death, Lincoln's body traveled from Washington, D.C., to his hometown of Springfield, Illinois. The funeral train generally followed the reverse route that Lincoln took when he traveled to Washington as president-elect in 1861.

Ohio Historical Society

Abraham Lincoln's catafalque in the Statehouse Rotunda, April 29, 1865

Ohio Historical Society

Atrium

Schooley Caldwell Associates of Columbus created the Atrium to connect the Statehouse and Senate Building in 1993.

Schooley Caldwell Associates

The construction of the Judiciary Annex in 1901 (present-day Senate Building) created an open courtyard between it and the east façade of the Ohio Statehouse. The yard was soon home to many varieties of birds, particularly pigeons that roosted along the exterior walls. According to Statehouse lore, when legislators crossed the courtyard, the crossing was best done at a run to avoid pigeon droppings—hence the name "Pigeon Run." Governor Asa Bushnell (1896–1900) noted early on that the construction of a building between the Statehouse and Annex would prove a great convenience. Nearly one hundred years passed before his suggestion became a reality; in 1993 the Atrium was constructed as part of the overall Capitol Square renovation.

Created in a style that is neither Greek revival nor Neo-Classical, the Atrium employs similar materials and scale of proportion that harmoniously complement the two historic buildings. The Atrium is a stately public space for hosting legislative breakfasts and luncheons, press conferences, swearing-in ceremonies, protests, awards, wedding receptions, and many other special events.

A stuffed pigeon atop the doorway is a tongue-in-cheek tribute to the old "Pigeon Run."

Second-level "catwalks" on each end of the Atrium allow visitors to walk between buildings while events are held on the first floor.

The Atrium is the site of special events, performances, and legislative events.

Map Room

The highlight of the Map Room is a marble map on the floor that shows Ohio's eighty-eight counties.

The Map Room is located directly below the Atrium and serves as a crossroads, or busy passageway, connecting the Statehouse to the Senate Building. Completed in 1993, the room gets its name from the twenty-by-twenty-foot marble map of Ohio on the center floor. As marble is not native to the state, colored varieties from around the world were chosen. The map is scaled at approximately eleven inches to ten miles, meaning a person five feet six inches tall would stand about sixty miles tall in relation to the map.

The Map Room features two bronze bas-relief sculptures, *Historic Classroom* and *Modern Classroom*, created by George Danhires of Kent, Ohio. The sculptures are gifts from the State Teachers Retirement System. The sculptor interpreted his works as portrayals of student experiences provided by dedicated educators and references to "cultural influences, important historical figures and Ohio educational innovations." Contrasting education of the past by showing old tools and methods with present techniques, including the teacher who signs "to learn," both reliefs feature Ohio objects (McGuffey Readers) and inventors, Orville and Wilbur Wright.

The Statehouse Museum Shop is located adjacent to the Map Room and promotes products made by Ohio artists and vendors, as well as Ohio-grown food and wine.

The State Teachers' Retirement System commissioned the sculptures Historic Classroom *and* Modern Classroom *by George Danhires.*

Ohio Government Telecommunications

53

Senate Building

The Neo-Classical style of the Judiciary Annex (now the Senate Building) complements the Greek revival style of the Statehouse.

Ohio Historical Society

Toward the end of the nineteenth century, state officials—particularly members of the judiciary—felt cramped among the swelling number of offices crowded into the Statehouse. Various proposals were put forth to expand the Statehouse by building wings or raising additional stories. After much deliberation, the General Assembly approved plans in 1897 for a new, freestanding Judiciary Annex located less than one hundred yards from the Statehouse on the east side of Capitol Square. Cincinnati architects Samuel Hannaford & Sons designed a Neo-Classical revival structure made from the same vein of Columbus limestone as the Statehouse. Unlike the Statehouse, construction on the Annex moved quickly, with the cornerstone in place by February 1899. Completed two years later, the Judiciary Annex housed the Supreme Court of Ohio, Clerk, Law Library, Attorney General, as well as the departments of Agriculture, Health Insurance, and Public Works.

The late-nineteenth-century design and execution of the Annex exemplified the state's status at a time when Ohio led the nation in economic prosperity and political prestige. Visitors then and now stare in awe of the Grand Stair Hall, the most impressive space in the building. The elegant stairs are crafted from white marble. Decorative gold leaf highlights many architectural elements throughout the building. Raphael and Charles Pedretti, Cincinnati's finest decorators and muralists, painted the ceiling with female figures representing the arts, manufacturing, agriculture, and justice. The figures surround a stained-glass skylight of the Great Seal of Ohio. Before its rediscovery during the 1990s renovation, the skylight had been covered inside and out with plywood for so long that no one knew it was there.

Thirty-one of Ohio's thirty-three state senators maintain their offices in the present-day Senate Building. (The Senate president and Senate minority leader's offices are located in the Statehouse.) The Annex houses three public hearing rooms and the Senate Majority and Minority conference rooms.

State senators listen to public input on pending legislation in three hearing rooms: the Finan Hearing Room and the North and South Hearing Rooms. The Finan Hearing Room (originally the Ohio Supreme Court Law Library) is named in honor of former Ohio Senate President Richard H. Finan, who successfully led the Capitol Square renovation. Senate pages

The Capitol Square Review and Advisory Board hung a Blue and Gold Star Service Flag on the Senate Building where it will remain until the conflicts in Iraq and Afghanistan are deemed resolved.

Visitors entering from the east side of Capitol Square are greeted at the Third Street Information Desk.

Ohio Government Telecommunications

The Grand Stair Hall of the Ohio Senate Building

Ohio Government Telecommunications

gather in the "bullpen" on the second-level mezzanine, which also provides additional seating for hearing attendees.

The North and South Hearing Rooms are the former Supreme Court Chambers. The hearing rooms are where ordinary citizens may participate directly in the lawmaking process by testifying before Senate committees on issues important to them. Hyperbole about "making your voice heard" becomes truth in these rooms—people speak, and senators listen.

The Majority and Minority Conference Rooms are used as caucus meeting spaces for Ohio's senators. Located on the northeast and southeast corners of the Senate Building, the Conference Rooms formerly served as deliberation chambers for justices when the building was the Judiciary Annex (1901–1974).

The ceiling murals by Cincinnati's Pedretti Brothers employ female figures to symbolize the arts, manufacturing, agriculture, and justice.

Ohio Government Telecommunications

The three-story Grand Stair Hall is the most impressive space in the Senate Building.

The Great Seal of the State of Ohio is used as a decorative element throughout the Senate Building.

Ohio Government Telecommunications

Sunlight enters the central Grand Stair Hall through an ornate skylight depicting the Great Seal of the State of Ohio.

Ohio Government Telecommunications

This ornate gate was discovered during the 1990s renovation. Its original location and purpose are unknown.

Ohio Government Telecommunications

59

The Richard H. Finan Hearing Room is named for the former Senate president who administered the 1990s restoration of the Ohio Statehouse and the Senate Building.

Ohio Government Telecommunications

One of two Senate Hearing Rooms located in the former Ohio Supreme Court Chambers.

Ohio Government
Telecommunications

The lobbies and offices of the Senate Majority and Minority Conference Rooms are located in the Senate Building. The lobbies are the only rooms decorated with aluminum leaf.

Ohio Government Telecommunications

Senate leaders meet in the Majority (left) and Minority (above) Conference Rooms.

Grounds and Monuments

A man poses with a Statehouse squirrel on the west lawn in 1902.

John and Janet Waldsmith

Shortly after construction began on the new Statehouse in 1839, the half-built foundation was covered over, and the grounds became an overgrown pasture. Throughout the nineteenth century, livestock grazed on the Statehouse lawn, earning Columbus the irreverent nickname "Cow Town," which lasted for many years.

Many other animals—particularly squirrels—also made the grounds of Capitol Square their home. Because they threatened the crops and livelihoods of early settlers, squirrels were hunted to near extinction in the first half of the nineteenth century. When they no longer posed a threat to agriculture, the creatures were sentimentalized and reintroduced downtown. City residents constructed a five-foot-square, four-foot-high Statehouse "squirrel house" with five rooms, front and rear porches, and operational doors and windows. From the 1880s to 1917, Columbus newspapers regularly reported on the antics of the Statehouse squirrel population.

Today, Capitol Square features well-maintained walkways in a beautifully landscaped setting of trees, plants, and flowers with numerous monuments commemorating important people and significant events in the state's history.

63

Samuel Smith Monument

A statue of Dr. Samuel Smith, dean of Starling Medical College, was placed in an unusual location adjacent to the sidewalk at Broad and High Streets in 1880.

John and Janet Waldsmith

A Columbus Planning Commission criticized many elements of the Samuel Smith Monument, prompting its removal from Capitol Square in 1915.

Columbus Metropolitan Library

The first monument on Capitol Square was dedicated by the City of Columbus on May 30, 1880, to honor local physician Samuel Smith. Sculpted by William Walcutt, the life-size statue pays tribute to the man who served as the dean of Starling Medical College (1849–1859) and the state's surgeon-general (1862–1864). Criticism by a 1908 Columbus Plan Commission report prompted the relocation of the Smith monument to Starling Loving Medical College in 1915. The statue subsequently moved to Washington Boulevard along the Scioto River in 1957; at some point it was stolen, damaged, recovered, and repaired. The Dr. Samuel Smith monument is presently located on The Ohio State University's medical complex.

These Are My Jewels

These Are My Jewels was unveiled on Ohio Day, September 14, 1893, at the World's Columbian Exposition in Chicago. More than fifty thousand people attended the unveiling ceremony, listening to speeches by Ohio Governor William McKinley, former President Rutherford B. Hayes, and General Roeliff Brinkerhoff, president of the Ohio State Archaeological and Historical Society, who conceived the idea for the statue:

Cincinnati's James W. McLaughlin designed the Ohio Building for the World's Columbian Exposition in Chicago. These Are My Jewels, *seen in the forecourt, was displayed at the Exposition before being moved to the Statehouse grounds.*

Paul V. Galvin Library, Illinois Institute of Technology

> As a whole there is no block of equal size upon the globe that is equal to Ohio in all that is essential for the abode of civilized men, but unfortunately we can not show Ohio as a whole, and when we look at our mines, or manufactures, or agriculture, or material products of any kind, there is no one thing of especial importance in which we are not surpassed by some other State, and so to show up Ohio in such a way as to compel attention and remembrance from the multitude, I suggest that we place a statue to represent Ohio's heroes, civic and military.
>
> It occurred to me that mind was more than matter, and persons are greater than things, and that States are not glorified by bigness or richness so much as by men, and then it was easy to show pre-eminence for Ohio, for in men of world wide renown Ohio is absolutely peerless among the States of the Union.

The Ohio Building was intended as a showcase of the state's industry, agriculture, art, and handiwork. Unfortunately, the building turned out to

These Are My Jewels

Statehouse visitors take a break in the 1930s at the monument These Are My Jewels, *on the northwest corner of Capitol Square.*

John and Janet Waldsmith

be an elaborate "comfort station," or public restroom, causing it to suffer many indignities.

Levi Tucker Scofield, a former Union officer, designed *These Are My Jewels.* Known primarily as an Ohio architect, Scofield created one other monument—the heroic *Sailors' and Soldiers' Monument* on Cleveland's Public Square.

These Are My Jewels features Cornelia, an allegorical figure from Roman history who represents Ohio. When visiting friends asked Cornelia to show them her finery and jewels, she cunningly presented her two sons announcing, "These are my jewels."

Scofield's original statue honored six Ohio's jewels in life-size bronze figures: General Ulysses S. Grant, General Phillip Sheridan, General William T. Sherman, Edwin M. Stanton, James A. Garfield, and Salmon P. Chase. When the monument was moved to the Statehouse grounds at the close of the Chicago exposition in 1894, a figure of former Ohio governor and former president Rutherford B. Hayes was added at the request of then-Ohio Governor William McKinley.

These Are My Jewels is located on the corner of Broad and High Streets on Capitol Square.

William McKinley Monument

William McKinley Monument

The statue of William McKinley faces the site of the former Neil House where Governor and Mrs. McKinley stayed while in Columbus. It is now the Huntington Center.

More than 50,000 people attended the unveiling of the McKinley Monument in 1906. Many injuries occurred as the crowd surged toward the monument to get pieces of ribbon and bunting for souvenirs.

Ohio Historical Society

Inscription

William McKinley

Twenty-Fifth President of the United States

Let us ever remember that our interest is in concord, not conflict, and that our real eminence rests in the victories of peace, not those of war.

Our earnest prayer is that god will graciously vouchsafe prosperity, happiness and peace to all our neighbors, and like blessings to all the peoples and the powers of earth.

The fame of such a man will shine like a beacon through the mists of ages—an object of reverence, of imitation, and of love.

The first two quotes are by William McKinley. The third, on the back of the monument, is from an address in the U.S. Senate by John Hay, Secretary of State under Presidents McKinley and Theodore Roosevelt.

Alice Roosevelt Longworth (lower, center)—the nation's darling fondly called "Princess Alice"— attended the unveiling of the McKinley Monument; her presence drew many additional spectators to the already enormous crowd.

Ohio Historical Society

Erected in 1906, the McKinley Monument honors Canton native William McKinley, former Ohio governor and twenty-fifth president of the United States. Five years earlier, an anarchist assassin shot President McKinley at the 1901 Pan-American Exposition in Buffalo; McKinley died eight days later.

The prominent New York sculptor H. A. MacNeil designed the sweeping semicircular monument featuring an elevated, life-size figure of McKinley flanked by two groups of figures representing Peace (the quick execution and resolution of the Spanish-American War) and Prosperity (the economic recovery from the Panic of 1893)—two of the president's greatest accomplishments.

An estimated fifty thousand people attended the dedication ceremony, including Alice Roosevelt Longworth, daughter of Theodore Roosevelt—McKinley's presidential successor. An American celebrity of her time, Mrs. Longworth's presence created pandemonium in the crowd, resulting in injuries to several onlookers.

Located on the west side of Capitol Square along High Street, the monument's location was reportedly chosen because each day on his way to work, Governor McKinley turned and waved to his invalid wife who lived at the Neil House across the street from the Statehouse.

Draped in a billowing garment and wearing the accoutrements of war, an angelic female figure holds an olive branch overhead and stares past the viewer toward a distant vista. Commissioned by the Woman's Relief Corps (WRC) of Ohio, the statue *Peace* honors Ohio men's and women's sacrifices and contributions to the Civil War. The WRC originated as an auxiliary to the Grand Army of the Republic (GAR), the largest and most influential organization of Union veterans.

Bruce Wilder Saville created this monument in 1923, not long after the end of World War I and the passage of the Nineteenth Amendment to the U.S. Constitution, which granted American women the right to vote. The statue is centrally located on the north side of Capitol Square along Broad Street.

Peace
Ohio Government
Telecommunications

Inscription

Commemorating the heroic sacrifices of Ohio's soldiers of the Civil War 1861–65 and the loyal women of that period.

Erected by the Woman's Relief Corps Department of Ohio

1923

When our country sent out the call to arms for the preservation of the Union Ohio sent more than three hundred thousand of her sons. . . They had the faith that right makes might and that faith dared to do their duty. . . This memorial is erected in grateful tribute to their devotion and self-sacrifice.

Men win glory in the fierce heat of conflict but the glory of Woman is more hardly won. . . Upon her falls the burden of maintaining the family and the home; nursing the sick and wounded and restoring the courage of the broken. She endures the suspense of battle without its exaltation. . . This memorial is erected in grateful tribute to the loyal women of 61–65 without whose help no victory—or lasting peace—could ever have been won.

Let us have peace.

Spirit of '98

Sculptor Frank L. Jirouch created the *Spirit of '98* in 1928 to commemorate the soldiers who fought in the Spanish-American War, Philippine Insurrection, and the China Relief Expedition (1898–1920).

Inscription

Erected by the State of Ohio to the honor and memory of the Ohio veterans of the Spanish-American War, Philippine Insurrection and the China Relief Expedition.

1898–1920

The cause which triumphed through their valor will live.

United Spanish War Veterans, 1898–1902 • Cuba, Philippine Islands, Porto Rico, U.S.A.

The Republic is secure so long as we continue to honor the memory of its defenders.

United Spanish War Veterans Memorial Commission appointed by Governor Vic Donahey. Authorized by the 87th General Assembly of Ohio.

Carmi A. Thompson • Charles F. Thompson • Ralph H. Carroll • Frank Auth • Thomas W. Jones • Frank D. Henderson • George F. Schlesinger • Ernest P. Hazard • George M. Forney

"We make immortal the principles for which they contended." —Edward S. Matthian, Commander, Department of Ohio, United Spanish War Veterans.

1928 by United Spanish War Veterans Memorial Commission (Ohio).

Cleveland sculptor and artist Frank L. Jirouch created a plaster maquette (right) of a Spanish-American War soldier in 1927 as a model for the life-size bronze statue, Spirit of '98 *(above).*

Ohio Historical Society History Collections, H 27133

Ohio World War Memorial

Inscription

Ohio World War Memorial

1917–1918

To justice in war and lasting peace after victory.

To the Armed Forces of the United States "with the going down of the sun and in the morning we shall remember them."

To the women of America in the World War. They served nobly in a just cause.

Authorized by an Act of the 88th General Assembly of Ohio. Myers Y. Cooper, Governor. Dedicated November 22, 1930. —Commission: Chas. W. Montgomery, Miss Pauline F. Abrams, Arthur W. Reynolds, Horace S. Keifer, Gilson D. Light, R. G. Ingersoll.

Designed by Arthur Ivone in 1930, the Ohio World War Memorial honors American soldiers—known as Doughboys—who served in World War I. The monument is located near the front entrance to the Statehouse on the west, High Street side.

Christopher Columbus Discovery Monument

In 1892, Monsignor Joseph Jessing commissioned a statue of Christopher Columbus for the Pontifical College Josephinum in Columbus, Ohio.

The statue of Christopher Columbus represents Columbus as "a man of thought and mind, rather than a man of action." The single figure is made of heavy sheet copper. Designed by sculptor Alphons Pelzer and executed by the company of William H. Mullins of Salem, Ohio, the statue stands nine feet high. After its completion, copies were ordered and delivered to Phillipsburg, New Jersey, and New Haven, Connecticut.

The statue was moved to the grounds of Capitol Square in 1932. Some sixty years later, Ohio's sister state, Liguria, Italy, donated the current base (featuring Ohio inventions and discoveries carved on Ligurian slate) and fountain. The monument was rededicated in 1992 as the Christopher Columbus Discovery Monument.

Inscription

BASE West side: Christopher Columbus, an Italian navigator, launched four voyages of discovery to the new world. East side: Donated by the Josephinum to the State of Ohio. This statue was relocated to Capitol Square. North side: The fountain honors Ohio's sister state bond with Liguria, Italy, the navigator's home. South side: The Pontifical College Josephinum commissioned this statue from the W. H. Mullins studio.

FOUNTAIN West side: **1492**. The spirit of discovery has the power to change the course of human history as demonstrated by the voyages of Christopher Columbus, whose imagination shattered the boundaries of the Western world. Modern history has been shaped by one man's courage to pursue a dream. **1892**. A dream shared by later generations who explored a vast continent where freedom and opportunity beckoned to those with the courage and imagination to venture westward. **1932**. Westward into Ohio came the successors to the spirit of Columbus, naming the capitol city of the new state after the man who symbolized the spirit of the frontier. . . **1992**. Frontiers explored by later generations of Ohioans extend beyond land and water to a new world whose potential remains to be unlocked by the spirit of discovery.

In the 1960s, a 1,200-car underground parking garage was added to Capitol Square. The garage lies under the Statehouse lawn. New entrances were added during the 1990s renovation.

Construction crews unload and install concrete for the roof deck of the new Statehouse underground parking facility, August 19, 1964.

State commissioners emphasized that public tax dollars were not used to construct the Statehouse parking garage, which opened in November 1964.

Ohio Veterans Plaza

Schooley Caldwell Associates

The Ohio Veterans Plaza *honors Ohio men and women who have served in the nation's armed forces since World War II to the present.*

The *Ohio Veterans Plaza* originated in an act of civil disobedience. Ohio Vietnam War veterans erected a hand-painted plywood sign on the Statehouse grounds in 1981 to memorialize their fallen comrades. The impromptu memorial stirred up controversy, but also generated empathy from fellow veterans in the Ohio General Assembly who pushed for legislation for a permanent Vietnam War monument. The plan evolved through many phases, eventually resulting in an inclusive memorial for past, present, and future Ohio veterans in both war and peace.

Designed by Columbus' Schooley Caldwell Associates, the *Ohio Veterans Plaza* was dedicated in August 1998 to honor Ohio men and women who have served our country from World War II to the present. More than sixty years had passed since the last veterans' memorial had been placed on Capitol Square. The *Ohio Veterans Plaza* features two curved, Ohio limestone walls inscribed with anonymous excerpts from veterans' letters home from World War II to the Gulf War. Designed as a main entrance into the east side of the Capitol, the plaza includes flowers and shrubbery, lighted fountains at each end, plus flag holders and inscribed names for each of Ohio's eighty-eight counties. The eighty-eight

Ohio county flags are posted for special occasions. Large lawns on each end recall parade grounds, and flagpoles at the center of the plaza display the U.S., Ohio, and POW-MIA flags. The center pole's base includes emblems of the U.S. Air Force, Army, Coast Guard, Marine Corps, and Navy.

Sample letters:

To the Reeses,

I was hoping to get glimpses of Saudi culture, but I've seen nothing yet except infinite expanses of desert. There is a constant wind blowing and the dust in the air makes visibility terrible. The wind blows little trails of sand across the dunes like spirits not at rest roaming the desert. It gives the illusion of a dream state. As a child, I learned about deserts. I'd never seen one except in movies and they don't even come within reach of the real thing. I feel like I've always been here. The place I sleep is my home. Ohio seems like a dream, intangible and far from my reach and I cling to it and memories of it because they are all I have. Memories can be trusted. The only other thing I trust is my M-16. I wonder how much I will change. I've seen what Nam did to men. I don't want to change. The hardest part of my life is coming.

Love to the family,
Brad

Dear Bevie,

Today I went to a man's funeral I didn't even know. As his body passed by with a draped flag over his casket, I had a lump in my throat and a certain pride that only a man in the Army feels when his fellow American and fellow soldier gives his life so that fellowship can survive.

As I raised my rifle to fire the 21 gun salute, a tear ran down my cheek. When taps was playing, both eyes had tears in them. I looked into the faces. Their faces asking, why? Being a soldier, I know why. And the man I didn't know lying in the flag-draped casket, he knew also and died for it. You're asking yourself why?

Because it's America.

As I was looking at the faces, one was looking at me. He saw the tears in my eyes. He smiled gently and nodded as if to tell me how he felt. Somehow, the red, white and blue seems to draw people together in times of despair. No matter who or what they are. We know, Bevie, because the Major we laid to rest was black.

Love,
Your Richard

1st Ohio Light Artillery, Battery A and the Statehouse Cannons

The 1st Ohio Light Artillery, Battery A is a group of American Civil War re-enactors that promotes the Ohio Statehouse as a place of civic involvement. In partnership with the Capitol Square Review and Advisory Board, Battery volunteers interpret Ohio's role in the Civil War through living history activities, including re-enactments of battle, camp, and civilian life in mid-nineteenth-century America. The encampments and activities take place at the Capitol and off-site re-enactments.

One of the highlights of Battery A demonstrations is the firing of the Statehouse cannons. Located on the corners of Capitol Square are two six-pounder cannons and two twelve-pounder Napoleons. The term "pounder" refers to the weight of the cannons' solid shot projectiles, which could be fired nearly one mile. Manufactured for Civil War use by Cincinnati's Miles Greenwood Foundry in 1864, the Statehouse cannons were likely never used in combat.

Civil War re-enactors from the 1st Ohio Light Artillery, Battery A pose with one of the Statehouse cannons on the Capitol steps.

One of four Civil War–era cannons on the grounds of Capitol Square

The city of Columbus celebrated its one-hundred-year anniversary in 1912 with the Statehouse draped in patriotic festoons for the occasion.

Ohio Historical Society

The Ohio Statehouse participated in the 1876 centennial celebration of American independence.

John and Janet Waldsmith

American flags on the west lawn of Capitol Square honor those killed in the September 11, 2001, attack on the United States.

1st Ohio Light Artillery, Battery A holds annual encampments on the Statehouse grounds. General Ulysses S. Grant (portrayed by a Statehouse Museum staff member) shakes hands with a Union soldier.

Capitol Square is the site of political rallies, protests, and performances.

About the Authors

Cheryl Straker holds a BA from the University of Scranton and an MA from The Ohio State University. She was a history curator at the Ohio Historical Society before presently heading up the Museum and Education division at the Capitol Square Review and Advisory Board. She has published articles in the *APT Bulletin: The Journal of Preservation Technology* and in *TIMELINE* (a publication of the Ohio Historical Society).

Chris Matheney has a passion for early American history and recreates various characters from the French and Indian War through the American Revolution. In 1998, he portrayed Major Robert Rogers in the award-winning History Channel documentary *Frontier: Legends of the Old Northwest,* as well as contributing historical research to the Ohio PBS documentary *Opening the Door West.* Holding a degree in Interpretive Programs, Chris is the historic site manager of the Ohio Statehouse, serving fifteen years with the Ohio Historical Society before joining Capitol Square's Ohio Statehouse Museum Education Center.